INDIAN INSPIRATIONS

CONTRIBUTIONS

BY

INDIA

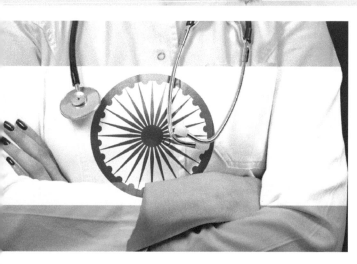

COMPILED

BY

MAYUR PARANJAPE

Tellwell Talent
www.tellwell.ca

ISBN
978-0-2288-5380-0 (Hardcover)
978-0-2288-5378-7 (Paperback)
978-0-2288-5379-4 (eBook)

AUTHOR

Author, photographer, clay artist, certified avian specialist, world traveller, nature lover, an active advocate of human rights, student of health studies, a patriot of India & a Canadian of Indian origin, Mayur Paranjape, is the author of Indian Inspirations: Facts and Contributions of India. He has a Master of Science in International Business from the University of Hertfordshire, United Kingdom. His inspiration lies in the devastating impact of colonialism on India and how well the country has still managed to score the rank as one of the potential superpowers while setting an example to other developing counterparts. In compiling this book, he aims at helping people understand India's contribution to the world.

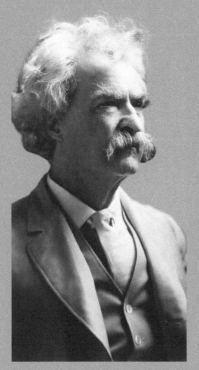

"India is, the cradle of the human race, the birthplace of human speech, the mother of history, the grandmother of legend, and the great grandmother of tradition. Our most valuable and most instructive materials in the history of man are treasured ... in India only."

— Mark Twain

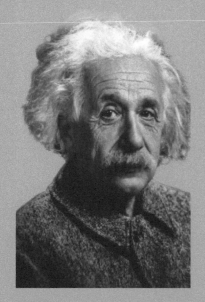

"We owe a lot to the Indians, who taught us how to count, without which no worthwhile scientific discovery could have been made."

— Albert Einstein

Indian Inspiration's

CONTRIBUTION'S

BY

INDIA

CHATURANGA
PRECURSOR TO THE MODERN CHESS

"One of the earlier games in history was a war game called "Chaturanga", a Sanskrit name for a battle formation mentioned in the Indian epic Mahabharata. Chaturanga flourished in northwestern India by the 7th century and is regarded as the earliest precursor of modern chess because it had two key features found in all later chess variants— different pieces had different powers (unlike checkers and go), and victory was based on one piece, the king of modern chess."

(Britannica).

CHAMPO

PREDECESSOR TO THE MODERN SHAMPOO

Although invented by G.D., Suffolk the first known mention of shampoo is from the 4th century B.C., when Greek historian "Strabo" wrote about India's practice of shampooing.

The word is from the Hindu word champo, meaning to massage or knead.

(Daily Press, 2003)

CHAMPO

PREDECESSOR TO THE MODERN SHAMPOO

Common ingredients used in making "Herbal Shampoos" are Gooseberries, Neem Leaves, Shikakai, Fenugreek, Ritha, Hibiscus and Aloevera.

AYURVEDA

"SCIENCE OF LIFE AND MOTHER OF ALL HEALING"

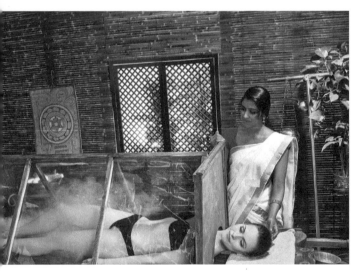
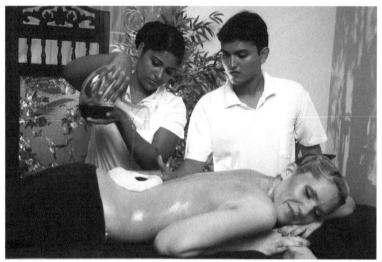

Ayurvedic (Botanical) knowledge originated in India

more than 5,000 years ago and is often called the

"Mother of All Healing."

AYURVEDA

"SCIENCE OF LIFE AND MOTHER OF ALL HEALING"

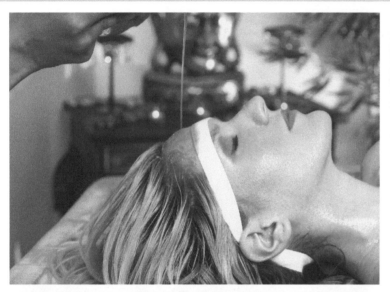
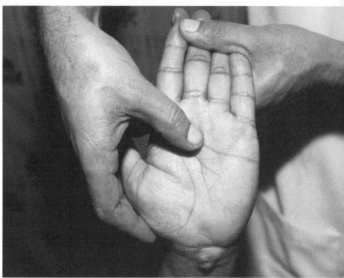

BUDDHISM

A philosophy & moral discipline, originating in
India in the 6th - 5th century BCE. It was
founded by the sage
"Siddhartha Gautama "

(Ancient History Encyclopedia)

BUDDHISM

Bodhgaya, India

Buddha Park, Sikkim, India

BUDDHA PARK, SIKKIM, INDIA

CASHMERE (KASHMIR) WOOL

The founder of the Kashmir wool industry is traditionally held to be the 15th-century ruler of Kashmir, Zayn-ul-Abidin, who employed weavers from Central Asia. The mention of woollen shawls made from this wool in Kashmir is found in several books between the 3rd century BCE and the 11th century BCE.

(Britannica)

CASHMERE (KASHMIR) WOOL

Sheep Pasturing, Kashmir, India

AGRICULTURAL HUB

India is a global agricultural powerhouse. It is the world's **largest producer** of milk, pulses, rice and spices, and has the world's largest cattle inventory, as well as the second largest area under wheat , sugarcane and sheep , goat meat, fresh fruits , vegetables, tea & cotton.

Third largest farmed fish producer in the world.

(WORLD BANK, 2019 / FAS/USDA 2020 / WORLD ATLAS)

AGRICULTURAL HUB

Rice plantation, State of Tamil Nadu, India

Banana Plantation - Vagamon , India

PHARMACY OF THE WORLD

The Indian pharmaceutical industry has an annual revenue of US$38 billion making it   the third largest in the world in terms of volume and 11th by value. It comprises over 3,000 pharmaceutical companies and over 10,500 manufacturing facilities.

India has the ability to produces drugs at around a third of the US costs and half of the European costs. Moreover, Indian pharmaceutical companies supply around 20 per cent of the worlds' generic's and 62 per cent of its vaccines.

(Deloitte, 2020)

INDAN SPACE RESEARCH ORGANIZATION (ISRO)

Department of Space, ISRO's states that the maiden mission to Moon, the Chandrayaan-1, has been an exemplary example of international cooperation with its international payloads. It has also earned several national and international laurels and was instrumental in the ISRO-NASA joint discovery of water molecules on the moon surface, unattained by any of the previous missions of such nature.

ISRO has launched International Satellites through Polar Satellite Launch Vehicle (PSLV) for 20 countries (Algeria, Argentina, Austria, Belgium, Canada, Denmark, France, Germany, Indonesia, Israel, Italy, Japan, Luxembourg, The Netherlands, Republic of Korea, Singapore, Switzerland, Turkey, United Kingdom and USA).

(Department of Space, Indian Space Research Organisation, 2020)

INDAN SPACE RESEARCH ORGANIZATION (ISRO)

WORLD'S LARGEST VACCINE PRODUCERS

60% OF WORLDS VACCINES ARE PRODUCED IN INDIA

(Reuters, 2020)

UNITED NATIONS PEACEKEEPING MISSIONS

India is the largest contributor of troops to United Nations Peacekeeping Missions.

More than 200,000 Indian troops have served in 49 of the 71 UNPKOs deployed so far.

(Ministry of External Affairs, Government of India, 2019)

(United Nations -Peacekeeping, 2019)

UNITED NATIONS PEACEKEEPING MISSIONS

In 2007, India became the first country to deploy an all-women contingent to a UN peacekeeping mission. The Formed Police Unit in Liberia provided 24-hour guard duty and conducted night patrols in the capital Monrovia and helped to build the capacity of the Liberian police.
UN Photo/Christopher Herwig

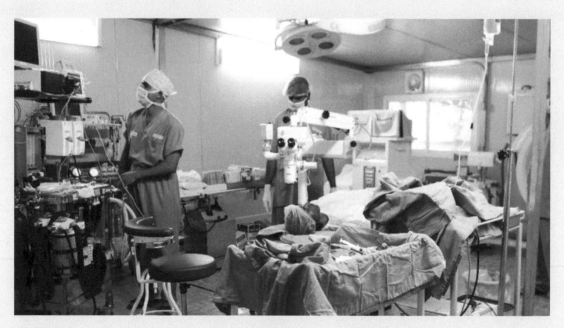

Indian doctors provide medical care to the local population in missions around the world, including in the Democratic Republic of the Congo.UN Photo/Marie Frechon

UNITED NATIONS SECURITY COUNCIL

INDIA BECAME ONE OF THE 10 NON PERMANENT MEMBERS OF THE UNSC IN JANUARY 2021

"G-20"
GROUP OF TWENTY NATIONS

INDIA IS A MEMBER OF THE GROUP

OF TWENTY (G20)

G- 20 IS THE PRIMARY FORUM FOR INTERNATIONAL
ECONOMIC COOPERATION AMONG ITS MEMBERS, THE
WORLD'S MAJOR ECONOMIES, REPRESENTING ALL
INHABITED CONTINENTS, 85% OF GLOBAL ECONOMIC
OUTPUT, TWO THIRDS OF THE WORLD'S POPULATION, AND
75% OF INTERNATIONAL TRADE.

(GLOBAL AFFAIRS CANADA, 2021)

INDIA
FIFTH LARGEST WORLD ECONOMY

3rd Largest - Purchasing Power Parity
World's One of the Largest Manufacturing HUBs

(DATABANK, WORLDBANK, 2019)

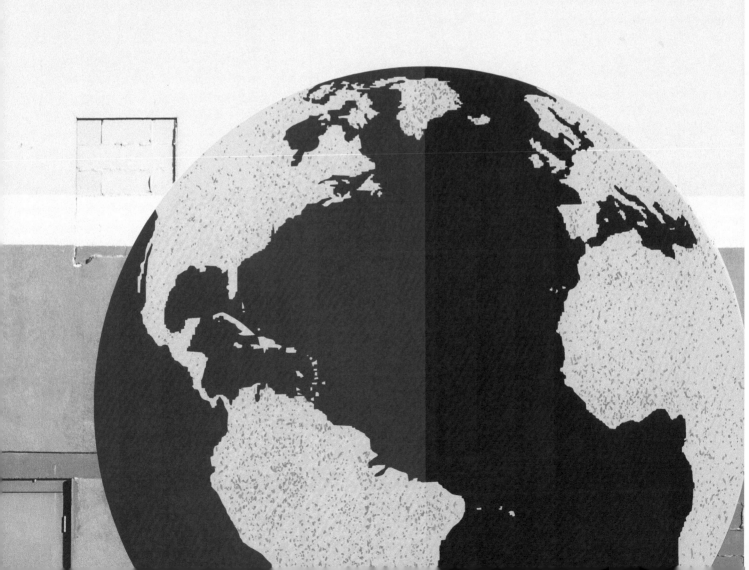

INDIA & THE ANTARCTIC TREATY SYSTEM

INDIA OFFICIALLY ACCEDED TO THE ANTARCTIC TREATY SYSTEM ON 1 AUGUST 1983. ON 12 SEPTEMBER 1983, THE COUNTRY BECAME THE FIFTEENTH CONSULTATIVE MEMBER OF THE ANTARCTIC TREATY, OFFERED TO COUNTRIES CONDUCTING SUBSTANTIAL RESEARCH ACTIVITIES.

(SECRETERIAT OF THE ANTARCTIC TREATY, 2021)

INDIA OPERATES 2 ANTARCTIC RESEARCH STATIONS

National Centre for Polar and Ocean Research, Ministry of Earth Sciences, Government of India.

BHARATI ANTARCTIC RESEARCH STATION, PHOTO BY -BOF ARTCHITEKTEN

BHARATI ANTARCTIC RESEARCH STATION, PHOTO BY -BOF ARTCHITEKTEN

YOGA
"THE ART OF LIVING"
INDIA'S GIFT TO THE WORLD

Yoga complex in Rishikesh, India

Foreign tourist learning the Art of Yoga in Rishikesh

PENTIUM MICROPROCESSORS

VINOD DHAM
INDIAN NATIONAL

FATHER OF PENTIUM CHIP LED TO THE
DEVELOPMENT OF INTEL MICROPROCESSOR

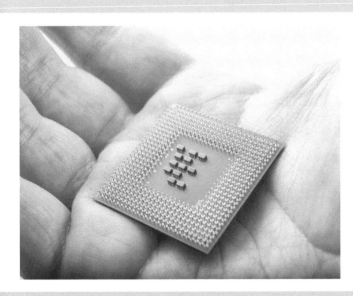 

UNIVERSAL FLASH DRIVE - USB

THIS INDIAN GUY **CREATED USB** IN 1996.

(Beebomco, 2018)

USB WAS DEVELOPED AND DEFINED BY AJAY V. BHATT, AN INDIAN-AMERICAN COMPUTER ARCHITECT

INDIA'S FOREIGN AID

IN THE INDIAN GOVERNMENT BUDGET OF YEAR 2019-2020 USD 1.32 BILLION WERE ALLOCATED FOR INDIA'S FOREIGN AID PROGRAMME. INDIAN AID RECEIVING COUNTRIES ARE BHUTAN, NEPAL, AFGHANISTAN, MAURITIUS, SEYCHELLES, MALDIVES, AFRICAN NATIONS, CARIBBEAN NATIONS AND A FEW OTHERS

DR.NARINDER KAPANY

FATHER OF FIBRE OPTICS

Meet
Father of Fibre Optics
DR. Narinder Singh Kapany

Born: 31st, October 1926,
Died: 4th, December 2020.

THE FATHER OF FIBRE OPTICS

REVOLUTIONIZED COMMUNICATION AND

HELPED PROVIDE THE UNDERPINNINGS OF THE

INTERNET INFRASTRUCTURE OF TODAY.

The Tribune, 2020

Sugar!

Sugar was first produced from sugarcane plants in Northern India sometime after the first century AD.

The derivation of the word "sugar" is thought to be from Sanskrit शर्करा (śarkarā), meaning "ground or candied sugar," originally "grit, gravel".

(BRITANICCA, 2021)

Sugarcane / Sunflower plantation - Karnataka, India

Sugarcane and Sesame - Haryana, India

NAMASTE

Namaste is actually a form of greeting that originated in India. It translates to, "I bow to you". But it is more than just a welcome greeting. It represents the warmth and amicability of Indians. It is also a form of showing respect and homage.

MARS ORBITOR MISSION
MANGALAYAN

INDIA'S SPACE PROBE ENTERED MARS ORBIT ON
24 SEPTEMBER 2014

CHINA /INDIA/ JAPAN/ RUSSIA SOVIET UNION/
UNITED ARAB EMIRATES/ UNITED KINGDOM/
UNITED STATES /EUROPEAN UNION ARE THE
ONLY SUCCESSFUL COUNTRIES SO FAR

(ISRO / NASA 2021).

OPERATION RAAHAT

In 2015 Yemen Crisis- 960 nationals from more than 41 countries including EU and the United States were evacuated in an operation by the **Indian Air Force and Air India**

(Washington Post, 2015)

MALABAR NAVY EXERCISE

INDIAN OCEAN

A TRILATERAL naval exercise involving the UNITED STATES, JAPAN and INDIA as permanent partners conducting drills annually since 1992 in the Indo Pacific ranging from fighter combat operations from aircraft carriers through maritime interdiction operations, anti-submarine warfare, diving salvage operations, amphibious operations, counter-piracy operations, cross–deck helicopter landings and anti–air warfare operations. "Quadrilateral Security Dialogue" and Inception of Australia is underway and formally agreed upon.

  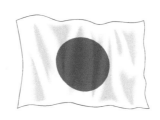 

(THE DIPLOMAT, 2018 / BLOOMBERG 2020)

INDIA HAS UNDENIABLY BEEN THE WORLD'S LARGEST SOURCE FOR IMMIGRANT PHYSICIANS

ACCORDING TO OECD, AROUND 69,000 INDIAN-TRAINED PHYSICIANS WORKED IN THE UNITED STATES, UNITED KINGDOM, CANADA, AND AUSTRALIA ALONE IN 2017

(MIGRATION POLICY INSTITUTE, 2020)

INDIA HAS ONE OF THE LARGEST

GOLD HOLDINGS

1	United States	8,133.5
2	Germany	3,362.4
—	International Monetary Fund	2,814.0
3	Italy	2,451.8
4	France	2,436.2
5	Russia	2,298.5
6	China	1,948.3
7	Switzerland	1,040.0
8	Japan	765.2
9	India	676.6
10	Netherlands	612.5

(US Global Investors, 2020)

DIAMOND CUTTING

The process of Diamond cutting has been known in the Indian Subcontinent as early as 6th century AD. A 6th century treatise Ratnapariksa, or Appreciation of Gems states that the best form in which to have the diamond is in its perfect natural octahedral crystal form, and not as a cut stone indicating that diamond cutting was widespread practice.

(UNIVERSITY OF PENNSYLVANIA MUSEUM OF ARCHAEOLOGY AND ANTHROPOLOGY, 1981)

INDIA GAVE CURRY TO THE WORLD

Curry originated in the Indian subcontinent and the word comes from the Indian Tamil word "Kari" meaning a sauce or soup to be eaten with rice

Curries form an important portion of dinner, in this instance, served on a Banana Leaf, South India

VOLUNTARY CONTRIBUTION
TO
WORLD HEALTH ORGANISATION

India falls in the largest 20 contributors of voluntary funds to WHO.

SWITZERLAND - 0.54%

INDIA - 0.46%

LUXEMBOURGH - 0.36%

CHINA - 0.2%

NEW ZEALAND - 0.14%

BRAZIL - 0.1%

(WHO,2019)

THE TAJ MAHAL

ONE OF THE SEVEN WONDERS OF THE WORLD

MOTHER TERESA
INDIAN of Albanian Descent

"By blood, I am Albanian.
By citizenship, an Indian.
By faith, I am a Catholic
nun."

MOTHER TERESA HOUSE

Mother Teresa room Interior

Mother Teresa House, Kolkata, India

DISCOVERY OF AMERICA

IN THE 15TH AND 16TH CENTURIES, EUROPEANS WANTED TO FIND SEA ROUTES TO THE FAR EAST. COLUMBUS WANTED TO FIND A NEW ROUTE TO INDIA, CHINA, JAPAN AND THE SPICE ISLANDS. IF HE COULD REACH THESE LANDS, HE WOULD BE ABLE TO BRING BACK RICH CARGOES OF SILKS AND SPICES. COLUMBUS KNEW THAT THE WORLD WAS ROUND AND REALIZED THAT BY SAILING WEST, INSTEAD OF EAST AROUND THE COAST OF AFRICA, AS OTHER EXPLORERS AT THE TIME WERE DOING - HE WOULD STILL REACH HIS DESTINATION.

AFTER SAILING ACROSS THE ATLANTIC OCEAN FOR 10 WEEKS, LAND WAS SIGHTED BY A SAILOR CALLED RODRIGO BERNAJO (ALTHOUGH COLUMBUS HIMSELF TOOK THE CREDIT FOR THIS). HE LANDED ON A SMALL ISLAND IN THE BAHAMAS, WHICH HE NAMED SAN SALVADOR. HE CLAIMED THE ISLAND FOR THE KING AND QUEEN OF SPAIN, ALTHOUGH IT WAS ALREADY POPULATED.COLUMBUS CALLED ALL THE PEOPLE HE MET IN THE ISLANDS 'INDIANS', BECAUSE HE WAS SURE THAT HE HAD REACHED THE INDIES.

ROYAL MUSEUMS GREENWICH, 2020

EXACT FORMULA FOR PIE(Π)

THE FIRST EXACT FORMULA FOR
Π, BASED ON INFINITE SERIES,
WAS DISCOVERED IN THE 14TH
CENTURY IN THE MADHAVA–
LEIBNIZ SERIES THAT WAS
DISCOVERED IN INDIAN
MATHEMATICS.

Π=3.14

ANDREWS, GEORGE E, ASKEY, RICHARD;

ROY, RANJAN (1999)

DALAI LAMA

His Holiness, the Dalai Lama, the exiled spiritual leader of Tibetan Buddhists, ran his government in exile from Dharmashala in Northern India, until his retirement.

Following the failed 1959 Tibetan uprising, the 14th Dalai Lama sought refuge in India. Indian Prime Minister Jawaharlal Nehru allowed in the Dalai Lama and the Tibetan government officials. The Dalai Lama has since lived in exile in McLeod Ganj, in the Kangra district of the State of Himachal Pradesh in northern India, where the Central Tibetan Administration is also established, where young kids are placed in Tibetian Central Villages. "Those between the ages of eighteen and thirty are placed in the Tibetan Transit School which offers the basic life skills required to acclimate to life in India."

(The Brooklyn Rail, 2008 / His Holiness the 14th Dalai Lama of Tibet)

Dharmshala, India - Home of His Holiness, Dalai Lama

Thiksey Monastery, Ladakh, India

26th May Science day in Switzerland is dedicated to Ex-Indian President, APJ Abdul Kalam

SENTINEL ISLANDS

UNION TERRITORY OF INDIA

North Sentinel Islands One of Worlds Most Protected islands only inhabited by the Indigenous Sentinelese people looked after by the Indian Government

SPICES
75 OF THE 109 SPICES ARE FROM INDIA

INDIA - HOME OF SPICES

WORLD'S LARGEST PRODUCER, CONSUMER AND EXPORTER OF SPICES

75 OF THE 109 VARIETIES LISTED BY THE INTERNATIONAL ORGANIZATION FOR STANDARDIZATION (ISO)

INDIA BRAND EQUITY FOUNDATION, 2021

Spices of India

NUCLEAR TRIAD

In 2018 India became the 6th Country To Have A Fully Operational Nuclear Triad - A three-sided military-force structure consisting of land-launched nuclear missiles, nuclear-missile-armed submarines, and strategic aircraft with nuclear bombs and missiles

The Eurasian Times, 2008

MINERAL RICH

India has the fourth largest coal reserves on earth and significant reserves of limestone, petroleum, diamonds, natural gas, chromite, titanium ore, and bauxite. The country accounts for over 12% of the world's thorium production and over 60% of global mica production. India is the leading producer of manganese ore.

(WORLDATLAS,2019)

MEDICAL TOURISM

36 ACCREDITED BY JOINT COMMISSION INTERNATIONAL, UNITED STATES.

THIRD MOST POPULAR DESTINATION FOR MEDICAL TOURISM IN 2015

INDIA HAS OVER 500+ ACCREDITED HEALTHCARE PROVIDERS (NABH) AND USES WORLD CLASS TECHNOLOGIES ON A PAR WITH THE WESTERN WORLD

DECCAN HERALD, 2019 / JOINT COMMISSION, USA

INDIA IS ONE OF THE FOUNDING MEMBERS OF

G - 20 - GROUP OF TWENTY

THE UNITED NATIONS

ASIAN DEVELOPMENT BANK

INTERNATIONAL MONETARY FUND

TOP TEN COUNTRIES BY FOREST AREA

1	Russian Federation
2	Brazil
3	Canada
4	United States of America
5	China
6	Australia
7	Democratic Republic of the Congo
8	Indonesia
9	Peru
10	India

GLOBAL FOREST RESOURCES ASSESSMENT

2020, FAO (UNITED NATIONS)

Forest's in Northern Sikkim, India

FINANCIAL ACTION TASK FORCE

India is 1 of the 37 members of the Financial Action Task Force (FATF) established in July 1989 by a Group of Seven (G-7) Summit in Paris that now examines and develops measures to combat money laundering, terrorist financing and financing of proliferation of weapons of mass destruction.

FAFT, 2020)

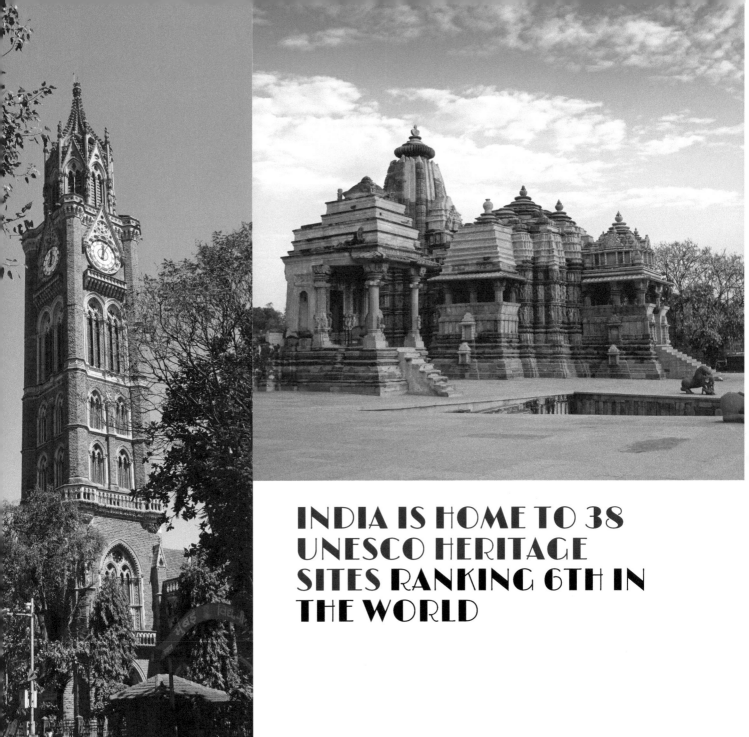

INDIA IS HOME TO 38 UNESCO HERITAGE SITES RANKING 6TH IN THE WORLD

WORLD'S FIRST HOSPITAL TRAIN

LIFE LINE EXPRESS INDIA

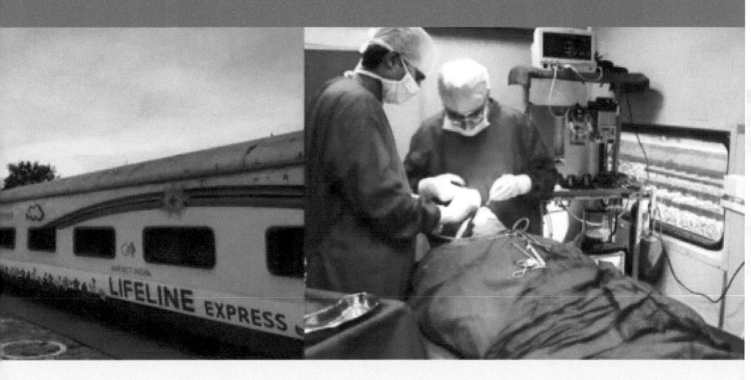

Travels across Rural & Remote India

FREE Medical Services to the Poor

800 Thousand surgeries over the past 25 years

Sanchari Pal, The Better India, 2017

WORLD WAR II

DURING WW2, INDIA PRODUCED THE LARGEST
VOLUNTEER ARMY IN WORLD HISTORY - 2.5
MILLION SOLDIERS

(BBC, 2015)

WORLD'S

PREAFERRED

OUTSOURCING DESTINATION

OUTSOURCING

According to a recent NASSCOM report, almost 50% of Fortune 500 companies directly or indirectly outsource critical business operations to India.

Example of a Software Park, India

Bagmane Tech Park, Bangalore, India

QUOTES ABOUT INDIA

WE OWE A LOT TO THE INDIANS, WHO TAUGHT US HOW TO COUNT, WITHOUT WHICH NO WORTHWHILE SCIENTIFIC DISCOVERY COULD HAVE BEEN MADE.

ALBERT EINSTEIN.

India conquered and dominated China culturally for 20 centuries without ever having to send a single soldier across her border.

Hu Shih.
(Former Chinese ambassador to USA)

India is the cradle of the human race, the birthplace of human speech, the mother of history, the grandmother of legend and the great grand mother of tradition. Mark Twain.

BIRD SPECIES

India ranks 9th in the world amongst countries with diverse BIRD species with over 1211 Bird species flourishing in India

Microsoft News, 2019

India's National Bird - The Peacock

REFUGEES IN INDIA

AROUND 195,000 REFUGEES WERE GRANTED ASYLUM IN INDIA IN 2019 ALONE COMPARED TO 101,000 BY CANADA, 54000 BY NORWAY,33000 BY BRAZIL

(UNHCR, 2020)

INDIA

ONE OF THE FEW COUNTRIES TO LEGALLY RECOGNIZE THIRD GENDER

As per the part III of Constitution of India and the laws made by the Parliament and the State Legislature, Central and State Governments are directed to grant legal recognition of gender identity such as male, female or as "THIRD GENDER"

In April 2014 - The Supreme Court of India declared transgender to be the third gender in Indian law

INDIA IS WORLDS LARGEST DEMOCRACY

UNITED STATES, JAPAN, BRAZIL AND MEXICO ARE

AMONGST THE OTHER LARGER DEMOCRACIES

Constitution of India allows the "Right to form Association", "Right to Express", "Right to Freedom".

The Supreme Court, Kolkata

STAR ALLIANCE

AIR INDIA - INDIA'S FLAG CARRIER IS ONE OF THE STAR ALLIANCE'S 26 MEMBER AIRLINES, A GROUP OF AIRLINES THAT OPERATE A FLEET OF APPROXIMATELY 5,033 AIRCRAFTS, SERVING MORE THAN 1,290 AIRPORTS IN 195 COUNTRIES ON MORE THAN 19,000 DAILY DEPARTURES

(Air India / Star Alliance, 2021)

ONE OF THE LARGEST FOREIGN EXCHANGE RESERVES

INDIA HOLDS AROUND 550 BILLION DOLLARS IN FOREIGN RESERVES

RANKING 5TH IN THE WORLD

WORLD NEEDS INDIA

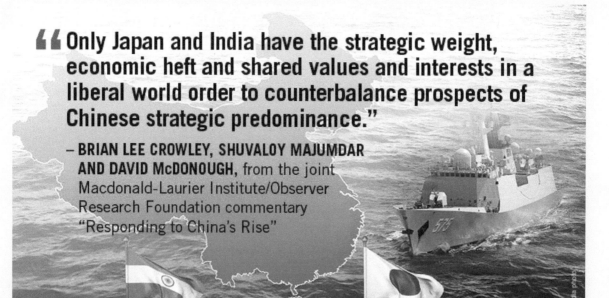

" Only Japan and India have the strategic weight, economic heft and shared values and interests in a liberal world order to counterbalance prospects of Chinese strategic predominance."

– BRIAN LEE CROWLEY, SHUVALOY MAJUMDAR AND DAVID McDONOUGH, from the joint Macdonald-Laurier Institute/Observer Research Foundation commentary "Responding to China's Rise"

Macdonald-Laurier Institute, 2017

GLOBAL LEADER IN PANDEMIC RESPONSE EFFORTS

"India provided critical medicines, diagnostic kits, ventilators and personal protective equipments to 150 countries during COVID-19 pandemic."

VACCINE FRIENDSHIP PROGRAMME

Vaccine Maitri

Country	Doses as grants	Country	Doses sold
Bangladesh	2M	Bangladesh	5M
Myanmar	2M	Brazil	2M
Nepal	1M	Nepal	2M
Sri Lanka	500K	Morocco	2M
Afghanistan	500K	Egypt	50K
Bhutan	150K	Algeria	50K
Maldives	100K	South Africa	1M
Mauritius	100K	Kuwait	200K
Barbados	100K	UAE	200K
Bahrain	100K		
Oman	100K		
Dominica	70K		
Seychelles	50K		
Dominican Republic	30K		

United Nations Secretary-General Antonio Guterres, 2021

VACCINE GIFT TO UNITED NATIONS PEACEKEEPERS

"Keeping in mind the UN Peacekeepers who operate in such difficult circumstances, India extended a GIFT of 200,000 doses of COVID -19 VACCINES for the UN PEACEKEEPERS in 12 missions around the world"

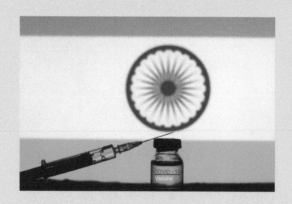

SOCIAL SECURITY AGREEMENTS WITH INDIA

Social Security Agreements with India

Belgium 01.09.2009	Germany 01.10.2009	Switzerland 29.01.2011	Denmark 01.05.2011	Luxembourg 01.06.2011
France 01.07.2011	South Korea 01.11.2011	Netherlands 01.12.2011	Hungary 01.04.2013	Finland 01.08.2014
Sweden 01.08.2014	Czech Republic 01.09.2014	Norway 01.03.2015	Austria 01.07.2015	Canada 01.08.2015
Australia 01.01.2016	Japan 16.11.2012	Portugal 04.03.2013	Quebec 26.11.2013	

Protects the interest of International Workers

Social security agreements benefit all workers moving across borders of the member nations.

The agreements ensures that periods of employment in other signatory countries are taken into account in granting the right to social benefits for migrant workers, dependant on the completion of a qualifying period

Ministry of Labor and Employment, Government of India, 2016

E-VISA POLICY OF INDIA

- All European Union citizens
- Albania
- Andorra
- Angola
- Antigua and Barbuda
- Argentina[3]
- Armenia
- Australia
- Azerbaijan
- Bahamas
- Barbados
- Belarus
- Belize
- Benin
- Bolivia
- Bosnia and Herzegovina
- Botswana
- Brazil
- Brunei
- Burundi
- Cambodia
- Cameroon
- Canada
- Cape Verde
- Chile
- China
- Colombia
- Comoros
- Costa Rica
- Cuba
- Djibouti
- Dominica
- Dominican Republic
- Ecuador
- El Salvador

- Eritrea
- Eswatini
- Fiji[3]
- Gabon
- Gambia
- Georgia
- Ghana
- Grenada
- Guatemala
- Guinea
- Guyana
- Haiti
- Honduras
- Hong Kong
- Iceland
- Indonesia[3]
- Iran
- Israel
- Ivory Coast
- Jamaica[3]
- Japan[2]
- Jordan
- Kazakhstan
- Kenya
- Kiribati[3]
- Kyrgyzstan
- Laos
- Lesotho
- Liberia
- Liechtenstein
- Macau
- Madagascar
- Malawi
- Malaysia
- Mali

- Marshall Islands[3]
- Mauritius[3]
- Mexico
- Micronesia[3]
- Moldova
- Monaco
- Mongolia
- Montenegro
- Mozambique[1]
- Myanmar[3]
- Namibia
- Nauru[3]
- New Zealand
  - Cook Islands[3]
  - Niue[3]
- Nicaragua
- Niger
- North Macedonia
- Norway
- Oman
- Palau[3]
- Palestine
- Panama
- Papua New Guinea[3]
- Paraguay
- Peru
- Philippines
- Qatar
- Russia[1]
- Rwanda
- Saint Kitts and Nevis
- Saint Lucia
- Saint Vincent and the Grenadines
- Samoa[3]
- San Marino

- Saudi Arabia
- Senegal
- Serbia
- Seychelles[3]
- Sierra Leone
- Singapore[2]
- Solomon Islands[3]
- South Africa[3]
- South Korea
- Sri Lanka[2]
- Suriname
- Switzerland
- Taiwan
- Tajikistan
- Tanzania
- Thailand
- Timor-Leste
- Tonga[3]
- Trinidad and Tobago
- Tuvalu[3]
- Uganda
- Ukraine[1]
- United Arab Emirates
- United Kingdom[1][17]
- United States[1]
- Uruguay[3]
- Uzbekistan
- Vanuatu[3]
- Vatican City
- Venezuela
- Vietnam
- Zambia
- Zimbabwe

AS OF 2021, CITIZENS OF THE FOLLOWING
COUNTRIES ARE ELIGIBLE TO APPLY FOR AN
ELECTRONIC VISA (E-VISA) AND ENJOY THE
WONDERS OF INDIA

INDIA

IS THE SECOND

LARGEST PRODUCER

OF SILK

(INTERNATIONAL SERICULTURE

COMMISION, 2021)

Women posing in Silk Attire "Saree"

ANDAMAN & NICOBAR ISLANDS

UNION TERRITORY OF INDIA

Permanently inhabited Union territory of India, around 2500 kms from the Indian Capital, far from the coast of mainland India, located in the Indian Ocean, close to Indonesia and Thailand

Andaman & Nicobar Islands
Union Territory of India

Andaman & Nicobar Islands
Union Territory of India

HOLY COW!

ONE OF THE LARGEST EXPORTERS OF BEEF

World Beef Exports: Ranking Of Countries

	World	10,657,000	
Rank	Country	2020	% Of World
1	Brazil	2,550,000	23.93%
2	Australia	1,400,000	13.14%
3	India	1,400,000	13.14%
4	United States	1,322,000	12.40%
5	Argentina	760,000	7.13%

Vietnam, China, Malaysia, Egypt, Indonesia, Iraq, Sri Lanka, Saudi Arabia, North Africa, West / East Asia are the largest Importers of Indian Beef.

INDIA GAVE "AUM" TO THE WORLD

It signifies the essence of the ultimate reality, universe, and consciousness

AUM is considered an original (primal) sound that rang out in the created universe

OM NAMAH SHIVAYA

A Glimpse into Northern India

A Glimpse into Southern India

A Glimpse into Eastern India

A Glimpse into Western India